Plant Secrets

Anna Claybourne

Raintree

www.raintreepublishers.co.uk

Visit our website to find out more information about Raintree books.

To order:
- ☎ Phone 44 (0) 1865 888112
- 🗎 Send a fax to 44 (0) 1865 314091
- 💻 Visit the Raintree bookshop at **www.raintreepublishers.co.uk** to browse our catalogue and order online.

First published in Great Britain by Raintree, Halley Court, Jordan Hill, Oxford OX2 8EJ, part of Harcourt Education.
Raintree is a registered trademark of Harcourt Education Ltd.

© Harcourt Education Ltd 2006
First published in paperback in 2007
The moral right of the proprietor has been asserted.

Editorial: Lucy Thunder and Harriet Milles
Design: Victoria Bevan and Philippa Baile
Illustrations: Philippa Baile
Picture Research: Melissa Allison and Fiona Orbell
Production: Camilla Smith

Originated by Dot Gradations
Printed and bound in China by WKT Company Limited

ISBN 1 844 21458 3 (hardback)
10 09 08 07 06
10 9 8 7 6 5 4 3 2 1

ISBN 1 844 43989 5 (paperback)
10 09 08 07
10 9 8 7 6 5 4 3 2 1

British Library Cataloguing in Publication Data
Claybourne, Anna
Plant Secrets: Plant life processes
571.2
A full catalogue record for this book is available from the British Library.

Acknowledgements
The publishers would like to thank the following for permission to reproduce photographs: Alamy p. 7 (Aidan Clayton), 26-27 (Jack Sullivan); Corbis pp. 14-15 (Douglas Peebles), 22-23 (Martin Harvey); DK Images pp. 10-11; Fairchild Tropical Botanic Garden p. 6; naturepl.com p. 21 (Geoff Dore); Oxford Scientific Films pp. 12-13 (Richard Packwood), 16-17 (Michele Burgess), 20, 24-25 (IFA-Bilderteam GMBH); Science Photo Library pp. 4-5 (Geoff Tompkinson), 8-9, (Ray Lacey), 9 (Sheila Terry), 18-19 (Gregory Dimijian), 23 (Paul Harcourt Davies)

Cover photograph of Venus fly trap reproduced with permission of Photolibrary.com/Kathie Atkinson

The publishers would like to thank Nancy Harris and Harold Pratt for their assistance in the preparation of this book.

Every effort has been made to contact copyright holders of any material reproduced in this book. Any omissions will be rectified in subsequent printings if notice is given to the publishers.

The paper used to print this book comes from sustainable resources.

Disclaimer
All the Internet addresses (URLs) given in this book were valid at the time of going to press. However, due to the dynamic nature of the Internet, some addresses may have changed, or sites may have changed or ceased to exist since publication. While the author and publishers regret any inconvenience this may cause readers, no responsibility for any such changes can be accepted by either the author or the publishers.

Contents

Some words are printed in bold, **like this**. You can find out what they mean on page 30. You can also look in the box at the bottom of the page where they first appear.

Plant zoo

Welcome to the greenhouse! It is a kind of zoo for plants. Here, visitors can see plants from all over the world. But most people only stay for an hour or two. In the life of a plant, that is nothing!

Plants need ▶
light to stay alive.
A greenhouse lets
in as much light
as possible.

To really see how plants live, you have to watch them carefully. Then you might see:

- a plant gobbling up a fly
- a squirting cucumber
- the world's biggest flower opening up.

So, what do plants really get up to? Read on to find out!

Plant parts

Seeds

Flowers

Leaves

Stem

Roots

Flower power

People wander past this plain green spike. They don't even notice it. But when everyone has gone home, the spike starts to open. The spike is actually a flower bud. It is the bud of one of the BIGGEST FLOWERS IN THE WORLD.

pollen yellow powder made by flowers that helps form seeds
seed part of a plant that can grow into a new plant

As the flower opens out, it begins to SMELL terrible. It smells like something bad at the back of your fridge. Because of this, it is called the "corpse flower". Plant scientists call it the "Titan arum".

The stink attracts flies. They love the rotting meat smell. As they land, the flies pick up a yellow powder called **pollen**. They carry it away to other corpse flowers. This helps the flower to make **seeds**.

Red hot chilli peppers

Once a flower has got some **pollen** from another flower, its petals drop off. Some of the visitors are sad when the flowers have gone.

But they should look more closely. Then they would see something where the flowers used to be. Slowly, the bottom of each flower is turning into a **fruit**.

Each of these ▶
chillies was
once a flower

fruit	part of a plant that contains seeds
reproduce	when a living thing makes copies of itself

The fruit on this plant is long and pointed. They start off green, and then turn red. They are hot, spicy chillies. Sometimes you eat them in sauces or spicy food.

The chillies are hiding another secret. Inside them are hundreds of **seeds**. Plants use seeds to make new plants. They **reproduce**. Each seed can grow into a new chilli plant.

seeds   fruit

◄Chillies are the fruit of the chilli plant. They contain chilli seeds.

Plant Fact

Chillies have a burning taste to try to stop animals from eating them.

Ready - aim - fire!

The visitors hurry past the cucumbers. "What's so interesting about cucumbers?" they mumble. But as the last man walks by, he feels a SPLAT! Something sticky has hit him in the middle of his back. The squirting cucumber has got him!

Plants want their **seeds** to find a good place to grow. So they spread them out, or **disperse** them. The squirting cucumber disperses its seeds by squirting slimy juice full of seeds. It can squirt this many metres away.

Other plants use other tricks to scatter their seeds. Some have very tasty **fruit**. Animals eat the fruit and carry the seeds away. Later the seeds come out in their droppings. Plants like dandelions have light fluffy seeds that blow away on the wind.

Plant Fact
Coconuts are "long-distance" seeds. By floating on oceans they can travel thousands of kilometres before reaching land.

disperse   to spread over a wide area

▲When a squirting cucumber is ready to release its seeds, it explodes. Seeds and slime fly through the air.

11

From tiny to towering

Some visitors hardly ever look down at the ground. If they did, they would see this little plant. They might think it was just a **weed**. In fact, it is a baby tree!

Most plants grow from **seeds**. A seed grows into a tiny **seedling**. It has just one **root** and one **stem**. Gradually it grows leaves and branches. Its stem gets thicker and stronger.

Even the tallest tree in the world grew from a seedling. It is called the redwood tree. But how did the tree get so big? What does it eat?

◄*This oak tree seedling is tiny now, but it could grow to be over 30 metres (100 feet) tall.*

root	part of a plant that reaches down into the soil
seedling	baby plant
stem	main stalk of a plant that branches and leaves grow from
weed	plant that a gardener or farmer wants to get rid of

◄ Redwood trees can grow up to 112 metres (370 feet) tall and they can live to be over 800 years old.

Plants need the Sun!

When visitors see this plant, they say, "It's just a bunch of leaves – boring!" But leaves are more than a nice green background for flowers and **fruit**. They are the "factories" where a plant makes its food.

This plant has ▶ no fruit or flowers – but its leaves are hard at work making food.

carbon dioxide	gas found in the air that is used by plants to make food
cell	tiny unit that living things are made up of
oxygen	gas found in the air and made by plants
photosynthesis	making food using sunlight

Each of a plant's leaves is made up of tiny units called **cells**. The cells use sunlight to combine water from the soil and **carbon dioxide** from the air. This makes a sugary food for the plant. Then the leaves release a gas called **oxygen**. This way of making food is called **photosynthesis**.

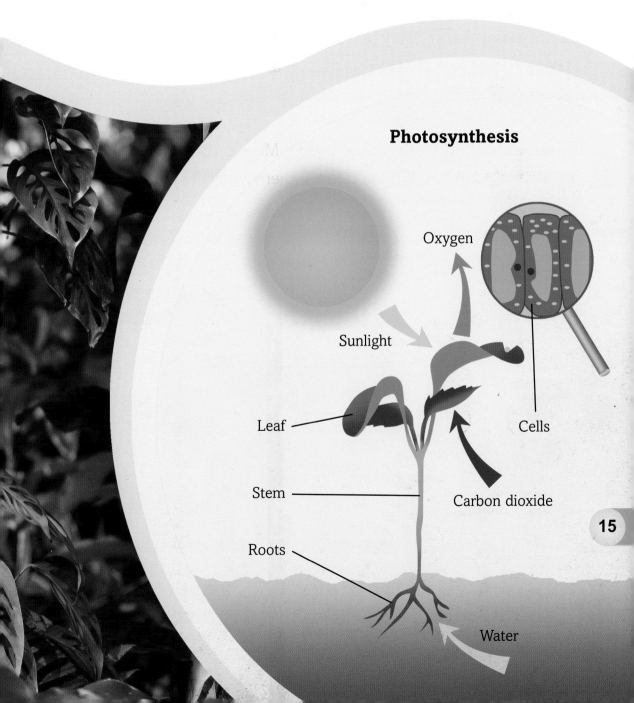

Photosynthesis

Oxygen

Sunlight

Cells

Leaf

Stem

Carbon dioxide

Roots

Water

Food for all

Some people might think plants are not as important as animals or humans. They'd be wrong! Without plants, we wouldn't exist.

Because of **photosynthesis**, plants do a very important job for life on Earth. They make plant matter – leaves, **stems**, **fruits**, and **roots**. This plant matter is the main food supply for most animals.

Even meat-eating animals need plants. Meat-eaters eat plant-eating animals. Without plants, there would be no plant-eating animals to eat.

Almost all the food ▶ on Earth exists because of plant photosynthesis. All animals rely on plants for their food.

carnivore	meat-eating animal (or plant)
herbivore	plant-eating animal
omnivore	animal that eats both plants and other animals

The food chain

Carnivores are meat-eating animals. They eat other animals.

Herbivores are plant-eating animals. They eat plants.

Omnivores eat both plants and other animals.

Plants make food using light from the Sun.

Plant Fact

*Besides making food, plants make **oxygen** gas. Animals breathe in oxygen to help their bodies work.*

Strangled!

The visitors really like this plant! "Isn't it a funny shape!" they say. "Look at that strange hole in the middle." Little do they know! This plant has a terrible secret. It is a strangler fig – and it is a killer!

The fig starts to grow between the branches of a rainforest tree. As it grows bigger, it drops long, dangling **roots** into the ground. It curls itself tightly around the tree. The fig's thick leaves block out all the sunlight from the tree's own leaves. The fig is gobbling up all the sun and air. The tree cannot make any food.

Then the fig wraps itself tighter and tighter around the tree. The poor "**host**" tree that the fig has strangled finally dies. It rots away. The strangler takes its place.

host plant that provides a home or food for another plant

The hollow space shows where the host-tree victim once stood.

Tough customers

Another family arrives at the greenhouse. They do not see the low, bushy plants by the door. That is, until they brush against them. "Ouch!" they shout. "Those **weeds** sting!"

The "weeds" are called nettles. In fact, weeds are no different from other plants. They are just plants gardeners do not like. They grow wherever they can. They are often very tough.

Nettles sting to stop animals and humans from eating them, or trying to pull them up. They also have super-strong **roots**. If you cut a nettle down, it will just grow again.

Roots are an important part of a plant. They suck up water from the soil. They also hold plants firmly in place.

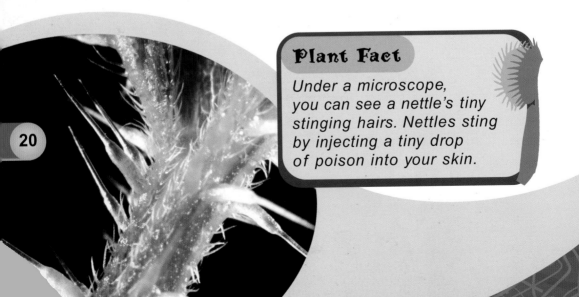

Plant Fact

Under a microscope, you can see a nettle's tiny stinging hairs. Nettles sting by injecting a tiny drop of poison into your skin.

◀ No matter how much you trample down nettles, new ones will grow. This is because they have a thick mat of underground roots.

21

Plants in disguise

One plant in the greenhouse hardly ever gets noticed. Visitors walk past it and think they have just seen a few stones.

In fact, those stones are the leaves of a very clever plant. The pebble plant is a type of **cactus**. It has two fat, round leaves that look just like stones. You can only tell that it is a plant when it flowers. Then, a bright white or yellow flower grows between its leaves.

The plant's disguise helps it to stay safe in its desert home. Passing animals would eat it if they knew how tasty it was. Hiding by looking like the surroundings is called **camouflage**.

It is not hard to see ▶ how pebble plants got their name.

22

cactus   type of plant found in dry places
camouflage   patterns or colours that help a plant blend

Plant Fact

*This bee orchid uses bees to spread its **pollen**. It attracts them by disguising itself to look like a bee!*

Hungry hunters

"Ooh, isn't this pretty, with its little frilly leaves?" says an old lady visitor. She is looking at a small plant. Then a fly buzzes past. It stops on one of the leaves. Suddenly, the leaf closes. The fly is gone!

This is a Venus fly trap. Its leaves work just like jaws. They are arranged in pairs with "teeth" along the edges. The fly trap is one of the few **carnivorous** plants. That means it eats meat.

If an insect touches the inside of the plant's "mouth", it closes tight. Powerful plant juices turn the insect into liquid. The liquid gets soaked up to give the plant extra food.

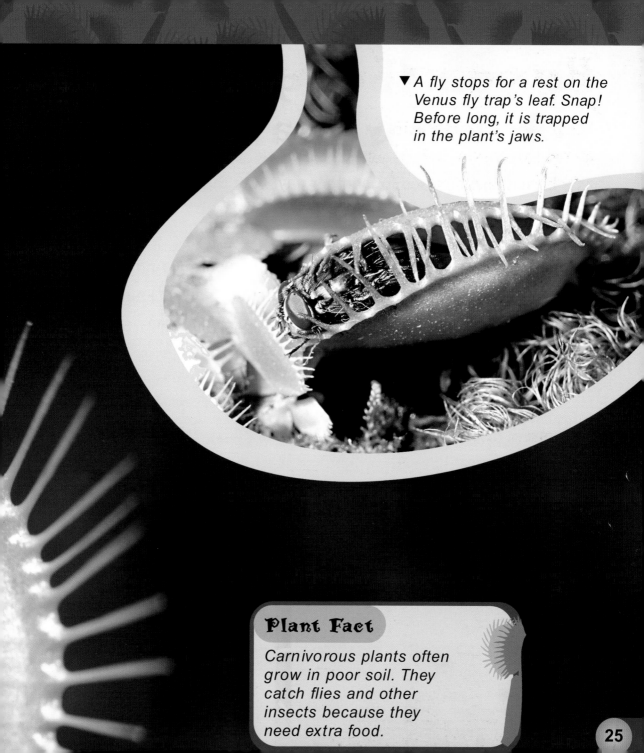

▼ A fly stops for a rest on the Venus fly trap's leaf. Snap! Before long, it is trapped in the plant's jaws.

Plant Fact

Carnivorous plants often grow in poor soil. They catch flies and other insects because they need extra food.

So you thought you knew plants!

The greenhouse is closed for another day ... but the plants inside are as busy as ever.

So now you know. Plants are not just green and boring. And they do not stay still. They can grow bigger than us. They live longer than us. They can poison us, and trick us. Some plants can even shoot at us! But most plants can help us.

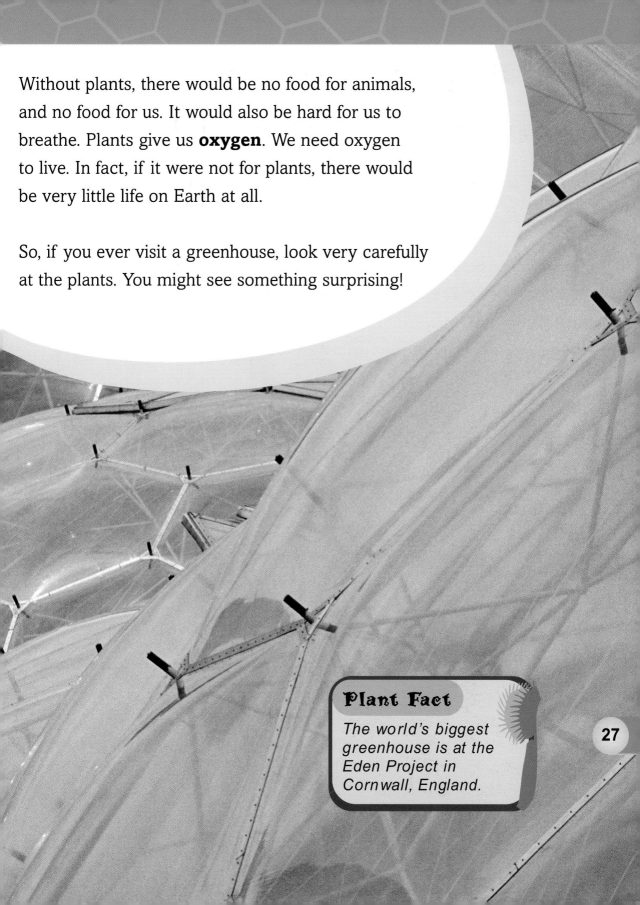

Without plants, there would be no food for animals, and no food for us. It would also be hard for us to breathe. Plants give us **oxygen**. We need oxygen to live. In fact, if it were not for plants, there would be very little life on Earth at all.

So, if you ever visit a greenhouse, look very carefully at the plants. You might see something surprising!

Plant Fact

The world's biggest greenhouse is at the Eden Project in Cornwall, England.

Plant parts

This plant is a sweet pea.

Pollen is usually carried from one flower to another. It is carried by the wind or by visiting insects.

Plants use their flowers to make new plants, or **reproduce**. Flowers contain pollen that helps to make **seeds**.

Leaves are where a plant makes food by **photosynthesis**.

Plant record-breakers

Fruits or seed pods contain seeds. Seeds can grow into new plants.

Biggest single flower: Rafflesia. *Grows to 1 metre (3 feet) across.*

Most poisonous plants: The castor bean plant and the rosary pea plant.

The biggest, heaviest plant: The giant sequoia tree. *A heavy as 35 blue whales!*

The **stem** holds the plant up. It carries water from the roots to the rest of the plant. In a tree, the stem is called the trunk.

Tallest plant: Redwood Tree. *Grows to about 112 metres (370 feet) tall.*

Fastest growing plant: Bamboo. *Grows over 1 metre (3 feet) per day.*

The **roots** anchor the plant in the soil. They reach out and soak up water and useful chemicals for the plant.

Oldest plant: A creosote bush in Joshua Tree National Park, California, United States. *May be over 10,000 years old.*

Glossary

cactus type of plant found in dry places. Cactuses often have spikes.

camouflage patterns or colours that help a plant blend in with its background. Pebble plants use camouflage.

carbon dioxide gas found in the air that is used by plants to make food. The bubbles in fizzy drinks are made of carbon dioxide.

carnivore meat-eating animal (or plant). Hunting animals like tigers and crocodiles are carnivorous.

cell tiny unit that living things are made up of. Plants, animals, and humans are all made of lots of cells.

disperse to spread over a wide area. Seeds often disperse on the wind.

fruit part of a plant that contains seeds. Apples, oranges, and strawberries are fruits.

herbivore plant-eating animal. Sheep are herbivores.

host plant that provides a home or food for another plant. An oak tree can be a host to a mistletoe plant.

omnivore animal that eats both plants and other animals. Bears, chimps, and most humans are omnivores.

oxygen gas found in the air and made by plants. Humans and animals need to breathe oxygen to stay alive.

photosynthesis making food using sunlight. Plants do this, so they need light to survive.

pollen yellow powder made by flowers that helps form seeds.

reproduce when a living thing makes copies of itself. All types of living things reproduce.

root part of a plant that reaches down into the soil. Roots anchor the plant in the soil. They soak up water and useful chemicals from the ground.

seedling baby plant. Even giant trees begin as small seedlings.

seed part of a plant that can grow into new plants. You can find seeds inside an apple.

stem main stalk of a plant that branches and leaves grow from. The stem carries water to the rest of the plant.

weed plant that a gardener or farmer wants to get rid of. Weeds are not different from other plants.

Want to know more?

Books to read

• *Fast Track Classics: The Day of the Triffids*, by John Wyndham and Pauline Francis (Evans Brothers, 2003)

• *The Revenge of the Green Planet: The Eden Project Book of Amazing Facts About Plants*, by Paul Spooner (Eden Books/Transworld, 2003)

• *Weird Wildlife: Plants*, by Anna Claybourne (Belitha Press, 2000)

Visit a greenhouse

• Royal Botanic Gardens, Kew, Richmond, Surrey TW9 3AB United Kingdom
www.rbgkew.org.uk

• The Eden Project, Bodelva, St Austell, Cornwall PL24 2SG United Kingdom
www.edenproject.com

• Australian National Botanic Gardens Clunies Ross Street, Acton, Canberra Australian Capital Territory, Australia
www.anbg.gov.au

It would be bad news for plants if the Sun stopped shining. Find out what this would be like by reading **The Day the Sun Went Out**.

Plants and other living things have special tricks for surviving. Read about how they do it in **Would You Survive?**

Index